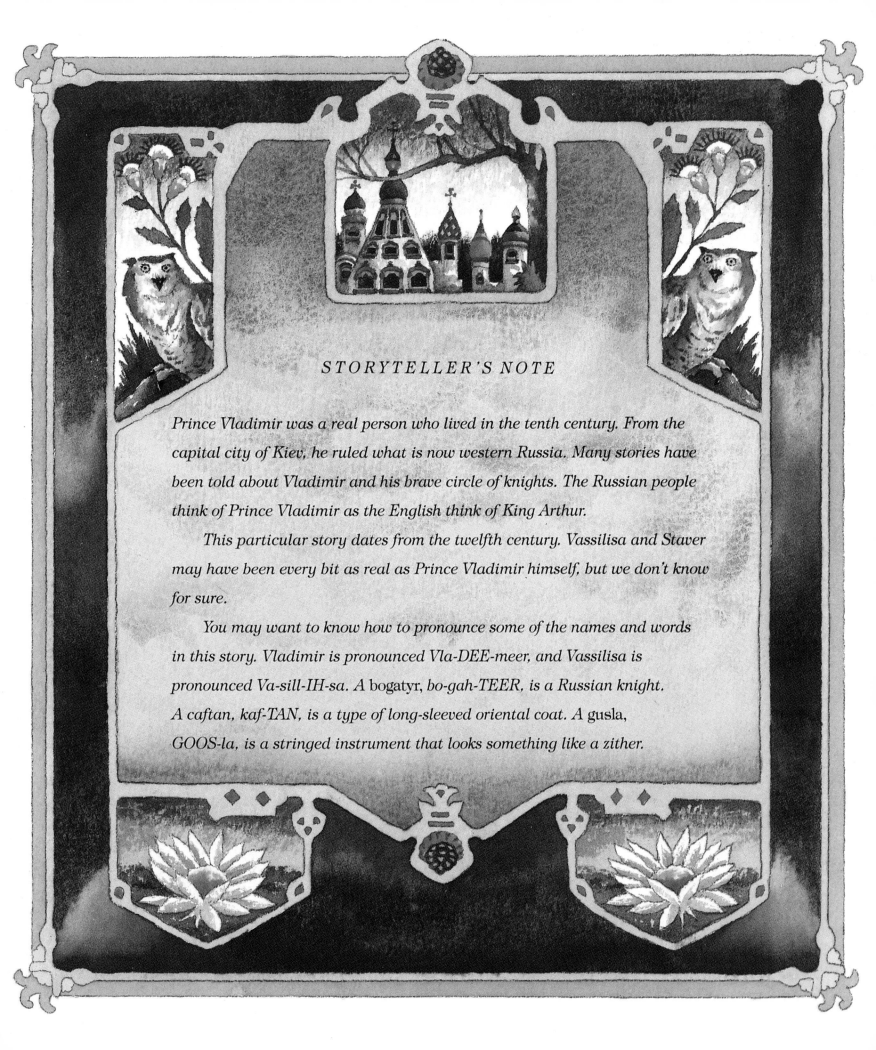

STORYTELLER'S NOTE

Prince Vladimir was a real person who lived in the tenth century. From the capital city of Kiev, he ruled what is now western Russia. Many stories have been told about Vladimir and his brave circle of knights. The Russian people think of Prince Vladimir as the English think of King Arthur.

This particular story dates from the twelfth century. Vassilisa and Staver may have been every bit as real as Prince Vladimir himself, but we don't know for sure.

You may want to know how to pronounce some of the names and words in this story. Vladimir is pronounced Vla-DEE-meer, and Vassilisa is pronounced Va-sill-IH-sa. A bogatyr, *bo-gah-TEER*, is a Russian knight. A caftan, *kaf-TAN*, is a type of long-sleeved oriental coat. A gusla, *GOOS-la*, is a stringed instrument that looks something like a zither.

HARCOURT BRACE & COMPANY
Orlando Atlanta Austin Boston San Francisco Chicago Dallas New York
Toronto London

VASSILISA THE WISE

A TALE OF MEDIEVAL RUSSIA

RETOLD BY
JOSEPHA SHERMAN

ILLUSTRATED BY
DANIEL SAN SOUCI

TO MY MOTHER
FOR THE LOVE, SUPPORT,
AND LAUGHTER

—J. S.

FOR JOSEPH AND
MARGARET ANDERSON

—D. S. S.

This edition is published by special arrangement with Harcourt Brace
& Company.

Vassilisa the Wise: A Tale of Medieval Russia by Josepha Sherman,
illustrated by Daniel San Souci. Text copyright © 1988 by Josepha Sherman;
illustrations copyright © 1988 by Daniel San Souci. Reprinted by permission
of Harcourt Brace & Company.

Printed in the United States of America

ISBN 0-15-302261-2

1 2 3 4 5 6 7 8 9 10   071   97 96 95 94 93

The paintings in this book were done in Holbein, Rembrandt, and Winsor & Newton watercolors on D'Arches paper.

Illuminated initial cap letters were drawn by the artist.

Designed by Joy Chu

ne fine night, mighty Prince Vladimir held a great feast at his golden court. Oh, what singing and dancing there was, what eating and drinking, what telling of tales! The whole palace rang with glee.

But one man did not laugh. One man did not sing or play his sweet-stringed *gusla* or drink the honey-rich mead. This man was Staver, the handsome young merchant-prince.

"Staver!" called Prince Vladimir. "Your playing of the *gusla* is finer than any minstrel's plunking. Play for us now!"

"Your pardon, Great Prince," said Staver politely, "but I do not feel like playing."

"What's this?" the Prince scolded him. "I've commanded song and merriment! Your silence is an insult! Why do you sit and brood, merchant? Are you jealous of my palace and my golden treasure?"

Staver had been thinking only of his new bride, his lovely Vassilisa. Had he not been ordered to the Prince's court, he never would have left her. Now he was longing for her, and he was homesick. That was the reason for his silence.

But as the Prince continued to taunt him, Staver grew angry, until at last he said exactly what was in his mind: "Why should I be jealous of you? I am a merchant, yes, but I've a finer treasure than you'll ever own, for all your royal crown! I speak of my wife, my own Vassilisa, who is fairer by far than any woman at your court!"

The air rang with cries of outrage from the women.

Vladimir reddened with anger. "What, Staver? Fairer than my own wife, Apraksiya? Fairer than my sweet niece, Zabava?"

"Ha! My Vassilisa makes them look like common milkmaids!"

"Oh!" gasped the Princess Apraksiya.

"I will not stay here and listen to such insults!" cried the Princess Zabava.

Staver was too angry to be still. "It's true! What's more, my Vassilisa is wise—wiser even than you, Great Prince!"

"Enough!" roared Prince Vladimir. "How dare you insult us! Guards! Throw this bragging fool into prison!"

Poor Staver! How he regretted his hasty words! But they could not be unsaid, and there he was in the Prince's dark dungeon.

Staver's serving man watched his master being cast into prison. Then he heard that Prince Vladimir was sending soldiers to bring Vassilisa by force to the royal court, so that all might see her. Quickly he took a horse and rode far and long until he came at last to Staver's estate.

Vassilisa was walking in the garden, her long golden hair brighter than the sun, her dark eyes keener than the falcon's.

"Terrible news!" cried the serving man. "Your husband has angered the Great Prince by boasting and has been thrown into prison! Worse, the Prince is sending soldiers to take you to the royal court by force!"

"That they shall never do," Vassilisa told him. "Nor shall my dear husband remain in prison. Many thanks for your warning, good servant. Tell me, of what did Staver boast?"

"Your beauty and your wit. He—he said you were wiser than the Prince himself!"

"Oh, I see! Go now and rest. I must think."

Vassilisa paced back and forth, her dark eyes flashing with worry. "Akh, Staver! Why were you so foolish?" She sighed. "And how am I to rescue you? Ransom? If you've angered him enough, the Prince will set a true prince's ransom on you, far beyond what we could pay. Force, then? Our servants couldn't defeat the whole royal army! What then, what then…?"

All at once Vassilisa smiled. "If I can't rescue my husband by gold or by force, then I'll rescue him by cunning!"

She called for her servants.

"Misha, my groom, saddle me the fastest horse on our estate! Sasha, my seamstress, make me the clothing of a Tartar nobleman!"

"A Tartar!" gasped Sasha.

The Tartar tribe was a part of the Horde, the mighty army of the Great Khan of the East. Even Prince Vladimir feared the power of the Horde.

"Quickly, Sasha! And you, my maids, must cut my long yellow hair. Don't weep; and hurry! I must be gone before the Prince's soldiers come!"

Prince Vladimir's soldiers were just approaching the estate of
Staver when they saw a horseman galloping toward them.

"Look at his clothing!" cried one soldier. "Look at the curving
bow he bears! That's a Tartar!"

"He's alone," said another. "Shall we kill him?"

"No, no! Don't you see how his caftan glints with gold? That's
a nobleman's son! If we kill him, we'll have the whole Horde down
about our ears!"

The horseman drew near to them.

"Where are you going, great *bogatyr*?" they called.

"To your royal court. And you?"

"To the estate of the merchant Staver, to seize his wife."

"Too late! She's gone!"

"What! Did the Horde capture her?"

"That's not for you to know! Go back to your Prince. Tell him I am coming as ambassador from the Horde. Tell him to be prepared to pay twelve years of golden tribute to the Horde!"

With that, Vassilisa rode off into the forest.

"Twelve years of tribute!" gasped Prince Vladimir when the news reached him. "We can't pay that! My poor people! If we don't pay, then we must fight the entire Horde! There must be a peaceful way out of this peril. Guard! Describe this Tartar ambassador."

"He's young, my Prince, slim as a boy, fair of face, and as well-spoken as a scholar. His father may be a Tartar, but his mother must be of our people, for his hair shone gold beneath his warrior's hat."

"I should think the rough court of the Khan would hold few charms for one like that! Perhaps we can bribe him…"

By the time the golden-haired ambassador arrived, the Prince was calm. "Good day, young *bogatyr*! And how are you named?"

"Vassili will do, Prince."

"That's no Tartar name. Surely your mother was of our people."

"She was. But don't expect that to soften my heart."

"Don't be so touchy, young Vassili! Come, sit and rest. You must be weary."

"The Horde does not allow weariness. Prince Vladimir, I have come to demand twelve years of golden tribute from you—and the hand of your niece, the Princess Zabava!"

Gasps of shock and surprise echoed in the great hall.

Zabava blushed red as a sunset and pulled at the Prince's sleeve. "Uncle!" she whispered. "I must speak with you!"

"Later, my dear."

"Uncle, that is no man!"

"What are you saying? He's the Tartar ambassador, Vassili!"

"That silvery voice?" Zabava whispered. "Those small and shapely hands? That is no man, my uncle—that is a woman!"

The Prince was doubtful, but thought it best to do a bit of checking. He said cheerfully, "Enough talk of business for now! Ambassador Vassili, we welcome you to the hospitality of our court. Tell me, young man, is it true that wrestling is a favorite sport of the Tartars?"

"It is."

"Would you care to amuse yourself now with some wrestling?"

"Why not?" said the ambassador calmly. "I would enjoy it."

Prince Vladimir called forth a champion, the tallest and strongest of warriors.

"Be careful!" whispered the Prince to his champion. "Don't kill him!"

But out in the courtyard, things happened differently than everyone expected. Each time the mighty warrior tried to catch Vassili, he caught only air! The slender Tartar was far too quick for him. At last the champion rushed at Vassili in fury—but the ambassador somehow stepped aside and caught him by the arm, sending him flying to land with a crash on the hard stone floor.

"You see?" hissed Vladimir to his niece.

"No, no, no! What you saw took cunning, not strength!" whispered Zabava fiercely. "That *is* a woman! Please, uncle, one more test!"

"Akh, very well!" He called to Vassili, "Our wrestler gave you no challenge at all! But our archers are truly talented. I see you carry a bow. Would you care to match your skill against theirs?"

The ambassador laughed. "I've been handling a bow since childhood! By all means let us test our skill!"

The Prince's twelve archers shot first, then Vassili, all of them
aiming at targets set up in the courtyard. The first time, nine archers
hit the mark. The second time, seven archers hit the mark. At last
only two archers were left, and one of them was Vassili.

"These targets are too easy to hit!" he laughed. "Come, do you
see that oak tree—that topmost branch with two leaves? You shoot
at one leaf, then I'll shoot at the other."

"Impossible—" began the other archer. But the Prince was

watching, so he shrugged, aimed very carefully, and shot. His arrow brushed the branch. "Impossible! Go ahead, Tartar!"

Vassili was already aiming, then shooting. His arrow clipped a leaf from the branch and went soaring over the palace wall!

Prince Vladimir hissed to his niece, "No woman could handle a bow like that!"

"She is a woman!" insisted Zabava, almost in tears.

"Very well, I'll settle this matter once and for all!"

Prince Vladimir called for his chessboard to be set up. It was a beautiful thing, inlaid with ivory and ebony, with chesspieces of silver and gold.

"Now, young Vassili, shall we play a game?" asked the Prince.

"Of course!" said Vassili. "I must warn you, I've been playing chess since childhood."

"Then would you play a game of chess for high stakes indeed?"

"What stakes?"

"If I win, no golden tribute will be paid. But if I lose, my city is yours." A shiver ran through the Prince as he said those words. But he could not unsay them.

"Done!" said Vassili.

They played chess all that day. Now it looked as though Vassili would win, now it looked as though the Prince would win. But just as the sun set and night came on, Vassili gave a cry of triumph.

"Checkmate!" he said. "The game is mine!"

The Prince sat in despair. "I meant only to help my people. But I have wagered that which was not mine to wager. Spare my city— take my life instead."

There was silence. Then the ambassador gave a little laugh. "Forget our wager! Keep your life—give me only the Princess Zabava!"

That night, at the feast to honor the Tartar ambassador, Vassili sat beside the Princess. She kept her head down and said nothing. But Vassili, too, sat with sad, thoughtful eyes.

"Why, Vassili!" said Prince Vladimir. "Is something not to your liking?"

"I was thinking," murmured Vassili very softly, "of prisoners in dark dungeon cells." But then he straightened. "I would hear music to cheer me."

"Done!" The Prince called for his musicians.

Without the smallest of smiles, Vassili listened to every minstrel, every singer, and every player of the sweet-stringed *gusla*. "Enough!" he cried at last.

"What's wrong?" asked the Prince.

"I've heard wolves howling in the woods that made sweeter sounds!"

The Prince turned red with anger. But what could he do? He didn't want to remind the ambassador of those twelve years of tribute.

Vassili continued, "I've heard that there is one man at your court who plays the *gusla* so sweetly that wild beasts grow tame."

"Staver!"

"Yes. Where is he? I would hear him play."

What could Prince Vladimir do? If he did not let Staver join them, the ambassador would certainly be offended. And if the ambassador was offended, he'd certainly remember the twelve years of tribute!

"Very well," the Prince mumbled.

In a short time Staver stood before them, pale and weary from his imprisonment.

At the sight of him, Vassili the Tartar ambassador cried out and hurried to his side. "Come, I will help you. You will sit beside me."

Staver was staring. "But you—you're—"

"Vassili, ambassador from the Tartar people. Yes, you do know me. We learned to read together as children. Now, eat something and drink something and then play your sweet-stringed *gusla* for me."

So Staver ate and drank, still staring at Vassili. Then he picked up his *gusla* and began to play. What he sang were praises of his wife. At the first words, Prince Vladimir tensed in anger. Those praises were what had started the quarrel in the first place. But Staver's music was so fine and his song so sweet, with love shining in every note, that all in that great hall became silent with wonder. The Prince forgot his anger.

When Staver was done, Vassili said, "Prince, your niece does not want to marry me. Very well! Give me this Staver to be my musician, and I will release the Princess!"

"Oh, do, Uncle, do!" pleaded Zabava.

But Prince Vladimir hesitated. "Staver may have been my prisoner. But he is not my slave. I cannot sell him."

"Give me Staver," said Vassili, "and I will go peacefully back with him to my own people. Give me Staver, and I will forget all about the twelve years of golden tribute!"

The Prince froze. "Staver, I must do what is best for my people. Very well, Vassili. He is yours."

"Not yet!" said Vassili, and hurried from the great hall before any could stop him.

In a short time he returned. Oh, but how different he looked! Gone were the Tartar caftan and leather boots. In their place was a lovely gown and soft little shoes. All that remained of Vassili the Tartar ambassador was the close-cropped golden hair.

"I was right!" cried Zabava.

"What is this?" gasped Prince Vladimir. "You are no man!"

"No, Great Prince!" laughed Staver happily. "This is not Vassili! This is Vassilisa, my own sweet wife!"

He ran to her there and then and hugged her, crying, "Oh, my love, will you ever forgive me? Will you ever forgive my foolish boasting?"

"Oh, I think the dungeon was punishment enough!"

"Akh, but where is your beautiful golden hair?"

"It was the rope that pulled you from that dungeon, love."

Prince Vladimir was so glad to be rid of the twelve years of golden tribute that he laughed till he nearly wept. "Oh, my dear Vassilisa, how you tricked me! You, a Tartar ambassador!"

"You believed me, did you not?"

"Oh, I did!" Prince Vladimir started to laugh all over again. "Akh, Staver, you were right! Your wife is lovely, and your wife is wise! And this once, this once, I admit she was indeed wiser than the Prince! Now come, you two. All is forgiven by me! And do you forgive your Prince? Good! Let us eat and drink and be joyful!"

nd they were!